Delectable Camping Recipes:

Quick and Easy-To-Cook Recipes for a Fun filled Outdoor Activities for Families and Friends (Grilling Recipes, Campfire Recipes, Foil Packet Recipes and Much More)

By

STEVE COLLINS

Delectable Camping Recipes

Copyright © 2019 by: *STEVE COLLINS*

ISBN-13: 978-1-950772-39-1
ISBN-10: 1-950772-39-X

All Rights Reserved. No part of this publication may be reproduced in any form or by any means, including scanning, photocopying, or otherwise without prior written permission of the copyright holder.

Disclaimer:

The information provided in this book is designed to provide helpful information on the subjects discussed. The publisher and author are not responsible for any specific health or allergy needs that may require medical supervision and are not liable for any damages or negative consequences from any treatment, action, application or preparation, to any person reading or following the information in this book.

Delectable Camping Recipes

Table of Contents

ENJOY THE FUN IN CAMPING 7
    BRIEF ON THINGS TO CONSIDER WHEN YOU GO CAMPING 8
    FIRST AID TIPS YOU NEED TO KNOW AS YOU GO CAMPING 9
RECIPES THAT YOU WILL ENJOY WHEN CAMPING 9
    DELECTABLE BREAKFAST AND BRUNCH 10
        Stuffed French toast 10
        Blintz Brunch Bake 10
        Spinach Quiche with Bacon 11
        Toad-in-the-Hole Bake 12
        Cheese & Pepper Omelet 14
        Sunday Brunch Bake 15
        Easy Ham & Eggs Benedict 16
        Cheesy Ham and Egg Sandwich 17
        Cheesy Egg-in-a-Bowl 18
        Overnight Stuffed French toast 19
        Easiest Soufflé Ever 20
        Walnut–Black Pepper Cookies 21
        Foil-Pack Chicken & Broccoli Dinner 22
        Crust less Bacon and Cheese Quiche 23
        Sky-High Brunch Bake 24
        Easiest Soufflé Ever 25
        Overnight Stuffed French toast 26

Cheesy Egg-in-a-Bowl 27

Mixed Nut Waldorf salad 28

Bacon Spinach Salad 29

Sunburst Fruit Salad 30

Easy Caramel Sticky Buns 31

Chocolate Chip-Banana Bread 32

Wild Berry-Oatmeal Cheesecake Muffins 33

Blintz Brunch Bake 35

Creamy Lemon Squares 36

DELECTABLE APPITIZER RECIPES 38

Chunky Vegetable Hummus Spread 38

Plantain Chips with Jicama and Avocado Salsa 39

Mini Cheeseburger Appetizers 40

Horseradish-Bacon Dip 41

Lime-Marinated Shrimp & Cheddar Appetizers 42

Easy Deviled Eggs 43

MIRACLE WHIP Creamy Spinach & Artichoke Dip 44

Basil & Tomato-Feta Bruschetta 45

Cheesy Spinach and Bacon Dip 46

Kielbasa Bites with Creamy Mustard Dipping Sauce 47

Rattlesnake Bite Hot Dog Appetizers 48

Bacon Appetizer Crescents 49

DELECTABLE CHICKEN RECIPES 50

Sweet Heat Grilled Chicken Sandwich 50

Grilled Chicken Quesadillas 51

Beer Can-Barbecue Chicken 52

Grilled White Chicken Pizza 53

Grilled "Cola-Q" Chicken 54

Grilled Chicken Flatbread 55

Delectable Camping Recipes

Cheesy Chicken & Veggie Mac 56

Butterflied Chicken, Beans & Corn Salad 57

Sweet BBQ Chicken Kabobs 58

DELECTABLE BBQ PORK CHOP AND PORK CHOP RECIPES 59

Barbecue Pork Chops with Mango Salsa 59

Classic BBQ Pork Chops 60

BBQ "Porkwich" 61

BBQ Smoked Pork Chops with Jicama Mixed Salad 62

Zesty Pork Chops and Grilled Vegetables 63

Saucy Barbecued Pork Chop Skillet 64

Cilantro-BBQ Grilled Pork Chops 65

BBQ Pork Wraps 66

Quick BBQ Pork Sandwiches 67

Pork Chops with Fully Loaded Smashed Potatoes 68

Bruschetta Pork Chops 69

Five-Pepper Pork Chop Skillet 70

Smothered Pork Chops 71

Pork Chop Stuffing Bake 72

French Onion-Pork Chop Skillet 73

30-Minute Italian Pork Chop Dinner 74

DELECTABLE DESSERT RECIPES 75

Rustic Chocolate-Cinnamon Bread Pudding 75

Quick Pear & Cranberry Crisp 76

Apple Crumble 77

PHILADELPHIA-Cherry Danish Dessert 78

Molten Chocolate Cakes 79

Meringue-Topped Southern Banana Pudding 80

Pumpkin Bread Pudding with Caramel Sauce 81

Warm Caramel Bananas 82

Gingerbread People 83

Chocolate-Candy Cane Cake 84

Fudge-Bottom Candy Crunch Pie 85

Gingerbread Pancakes with Warm Lemon Sauce 86

Pumpkin Bread Pudding with Caramel Sauce 87

Chocolate Chunk Pumpkin Bread 88

Double-Chocolate Filled Strawberries 89

Vanilla-Almond Fruit Tart 90

Lemon-Blueberry Crumb Bars 91

Creamy Layered Fruit Sensation 92

Made-Over Triple-Chocolate Dream Pie 93

Chocolate Dunk Cookies 94

Low-Fat Chocolate-Banana Parfaits 95

DELECTABLE SIDE DISH RECIPE 96

Hoisin Honey Chicken Wings 96

Slow-Roasted Potato Salad with Bacon 97

Mexican Spiced Corn Packets 98

Potato Salad 99

Delightfully Light Green Bean Casserole 100

Baked Pesto Chicken Sandwich 101

Slow Cooker Honey Apple Challah Stuffing 102

Layered Taco Dip 103

Vegetarian Black Bean Soup 104

Homemade Spinach Pizza Rolls 105

CONCLUSION 107

ENJOY THE FUN IN CAMPING

Don't let yourself to be intimidated; going camping is simple, almost unbelievably cheap and a lot of fun. Those group trips usually take a little encouragement.

Me and my family like the idea of going somewhere pretty, but worry about being bored, uncomfortable or just spending too much money. But I keep tell them to think of going camping like having a barbecue or a dinner party, just somewhere amazingly beautiful.

However, it's the most quality moment we spend together as a family, actually enjoying each other's company and with no cell service, phones are off, minds are present and the rest of the world just sort of fades away.

Being outside home and the only thing that matters now is having a good time. Remember, you are going to hit some bumps along the camping road just treat them as learning experiences and apply common sense and logic and you'll be ok.

Finally, make your first experience easy and short (two days, one night) and build from there. In the other hand, if you think you might like backpacking, I suggest you try day hikes first. If you want to spend time on the water, then you have to rent a canoe for an afternoon and see what that's like. So I advise you start small, get used to the outdoors, learn what you do and don't like and just keep growing from there.

BRIEF ON THINGS TO CONSIDER WHEN YOU GO CAMPING

A lot of people wish they knew how to have the best time when they go camping. Yet there is not a lot of knowledge on the internet on the best way to enjoy yourself while you camp.

Here are the basic guide a first timers needs to know.

First, you have to let all the members of your family/friends have a hand in picking your campsite (discuss which state you would most like to visit).

If you are traveling with kids, I suggest you consider staying at a campground that is specifically designated for families.

Make sure you know what is available in the area around your campsite. This is important if you have kids, but adults need a little entertainment as well!

However, if you are camping and the weather is starting to rise significantly, then you tale the coolers that you have with you and put them somewhere in the shade.

Make sure you pour out any water that has accumulated in your freezer each day.

Try to bring along with you some plastic totes or canisters so you can store any food products you have opened. This will prevent animal encroachment.

When you are packing your clothing for a camping trip, I suggest you remember that it is best to dress in layers. Make sure you take along a rain coat that you can put on top of every other layer to keep you dry if it rains.

I will advise you carry water that is clean if you will not have access to a safe spring or to clean tap water when you're camping.

As long as you adhere to the advice that was outlined from this article everything should work out for you while you go camping. Camping is a once in a lifetime experience, and will help you relax.

FIRST AID TIPS YOU NEED TO KNOW AS YOU GO CAMPING

1. Make sure you take a First Aid class and a CPR class (Note: keep current on this information)
2. Make sure you keep supplies in a well-marked, durable, waterproof container
3. Make sure you keep the contents organized
4. Make sure you know how to use everything in your first aid kit
5. Make sure to inspect content often, re-supply as needed
6. Finally, you keep readily available at all times

RECIPES THAT YOU WILL ENJOY WHEN CAMPING

DELECTABLE BREAKFAST AND BRUNCH

Stuffed French toast

Ingredients:

4 eggs

8 slices OF cinnamon-raisin bread

4 Teaspoons of sugar

½ cup of PHILADELPHIA Cream Cheese Spread

4 tablespoons of maple-flavored or pancake syrup

16 slices of OSCAR MAYER Deli Fresh Honey Ham

4 tablespoons of milk

Directions:

1. First, you spread bread slices with cream cheese spread; fill with ham to make 4 sandwiches.
2. After which you lightly press edges together to seal.
3. After that, you beat eggs, milk and sugar with fork in pie plate until blended.
4. At this point, you dip sandwiches in egg mixture, turning over to evenly moisten both sides.
5. Then you spray large nonstick skillet with cooking spray; heat on medium heat.
6. This is when you add sandwiches and cook for 2 min. on each side or until golden brown on both sides.
7. Finally, you serve with syrup.

Blintz Brunch Bake
Ingredients:

1 container (about 15 oz.) POLLY-O Natural Part Skim Ricotta Cheese

¾ cup of sugar (divided)

1 cup of flour

1 Tablespoon of CALUMET Baking Powder

2 pkg. (about 8 oz. each) PHILADELPHIA Neufchatel Cheese, softened

5 eggs (divided)

2 teaspoons of zest and 3 Tablespoons of juice from 1 lemon

¾ cup of butter or margarine (melted)

¼ cup of milk

Directions:

1. First, you heat oven to a temperature of 325°F.
2. After which you beat Neufchatel, 1/4 cup sugar, ricotta, 2 eggs, lemon zest and juice in large bowl with mixer until blended.
3. After that, you whisk remaining eggs, butter, milk, sugar, flour and baking powder in separate bowl until blended.
4. Then you spread 1/3 of the batter onto bottom of 13x9-inch baking dish sprayed with cooking spray.
5. At this point, you cover with Neufchatel mixture, then remaining batter.
6. Finally, you bake for about 45 min. or until center is set.

Spinach Quiche with Bacon
Ingredients:

2 cups of KRAFT Shredded Sharp Cheddar Cheese

1 pkg. (about 10 oz.) frozen chopped spinach (cooked, well drained)

2 eggs (beaten)

Dash pepper

1 ready-to-use refrigerated pie crust (about 1/2 of 15-oz. pkg.)

2 Tablespoons of flour

1 cup of milk

    3 slices of OSCAR MAYER Bacon (cooked, crumbled)

½ teaspoon of salt

Directions:

1. First, you heat oven to a temperature of 350°F.
2. After which you line 9-inch pie plate with crust; flute edge.
3. After that, you toss cheese with flour in medium bowl.
4. Then you add remaining ingredients and pour into crust.
5. Finally, you bake for 1 hour or until knife inserted in center comes out clean.

Toad-in-the-Hole Bake
Ingredients:

2 Tablespoons of margarine (softened)

4 slices of OSCAR MAYER Bacon (cooked, crumbled)

16 slices of bread

1 ½ cups of KRAFT 2% Milk Shredded Cheddar Cheese, divided

8 eggs

Directions:

1. In the meantime, you heat oven to a temperature of 400°F.
2. After which you cut hole in center of each of the 8 bread slices, using 1-1/2-inch cookie cutter or rim of drinking glass.
3. After that, you discard removed bread circles or reserve for another use.
4. Then you spread remaining bread slices with margarine.
5. At this point, you place, margarine-sides down, in 13x9-inch baking dish; sprinkle with 1 cup cheese.
6. Furthermore, you top with cut-out bread slices to make 8 sandwiches.
7. This is when you break 1 egg into each hole.
8. Then you sprinkle with remaining ½ cup of cheese and the bacon.
9. Finally, you bake for about 15 to 20 min. or until cheese is melted and eggs are set.

Cheese & Pepper Omelet
Ingredients:

4 egg whites
1 green pepper (chopped)
½ cup of chopped onions
½ cup of TACO BELL® Thick & Chunky Salsa
4 whole eggs
¼ cup of water
1 yellow pepper (chopped)
½ cup of KRAFT 2% Milk Shredded Mild Cheddar Cheese

Ingredients:

1. First, you beat whole eggs, egg whites and water with whisk until well blended.
2. After which you cook vegetables in large nonstick skillet sprayed with cooking spray on medium-high heat for 5 min. or until crisp-tender.
3. After that, you remove from skillet and set aside.
4. Then you add eggs to skillet; cover and cook for 6 min.
5. Furthermore, you top half of omelet with pepper mixture and cheese; fold in half.
6. After which you cook, covered, for 3 min. or until cheese is melted.
7. Finally, you serve topped with salsa.

Sunday Brunch Bake

Ingredients:

2/3 cup of BREAKSTONE'S or KNUDSEN Sour Cream

2 cups of sliced fresh mushrooms

2 pkg. (about 8 oz. each) KRAFT Finely Shredded Triple Cheddar Cheese

2 doz. eggs

2 pkg. (about 16 oz. each) breakfast pork sausage

   2 onion (chopped)

   4 tomatoes (chopped)

Directions:

1. First, you heat oven to a temperature of 400°F.
2. After which you beat eggs and sour cream with whisk until blended.
3. After that, you pour into 13x9-inch baking dish sprayed with cooking spray.
4. Bake for about 10 min. or until egg mixture is softly set.
5. In the meantime, you cook sausage, mushrooms and onions in large skillet on medium heat 6 to 8 min. or until sausage is done, stirring occasionally.
6. Drain and reduce oven temperature to 325°F.
7. At this point, you spoon tomatoes over egg layer; cover with sausage mixture and cheese.
8. Finally, you bake for 30 min. or until center is set.

Easy Ham & Eggs Benedict

Ingredients:

½ cup of KRAFT Light Mayo Reduced Fat Mayonnaise

4 English muffins (split, toasted)

8 large eggs (poached)

½ cup of plain nonfat yogurt

2 teaspoons of yellow mustard

24 slices of OSCAR MAYER Deli Fresh Smoked Ham

Directions:

1. First, you cook yogurt, mayo and mustard in saucepan on low heat 5 min. or until heated through, stirring constantly.
2. Then you top muffin halves with ham, eggs and sauce.

Cheesy Ham and Egg Sandwich

Ingredients:

2 slices of white bread

1 KRAFT Singles

1 eggs

1 tablespoons of KRAFT Real Mayo Mayonnaise

1 slices of OSCAR MAYER Smoked Ham

Directions:

1. First, you heat skillet sprayed with cooking spray on medium heat.
2. After which you add egg; cook for 4 min. or until white is set and yolk is cooked to desired doneness.
3. After that, you remove from skillet and spread bread slices with mayo.
4. Then you place 1 bread slice, mayo-side down in skillet; top with ham, egg, Singles and remaining bread slice, mayo-side up.
5. Finally, you cook for 2 min. on each side or until golden brown on both sides.

Cheesy Egg-in-a-Bowl

Ingredients:

12 slices of cooked OSCAR MAYER Bacon (divided)
1 tablespoons of chopped fresh chives

6 dinner rolls (about 3-1/2 inch)

6 oz. VELVEETA (cut into 6 slices)

6 eggs

Directions:

1. First, you heat oven to a temperature of 375°F.
2. After which you cut tops off rolls; set aside.
3. After that, you make 1-inch-deep indentation in center of bottom half of each roll.
4. At this point, you crumble 6 bacon slices; sprinkle into bread bowls.
5. Then you top with VELVEETA and slip 1 cracked egg into each bowl; place on baking sheet.
6. Furthermore, you bake for about 20 to 25 min. or until egg whites are completely set and yolks begin to thicken but are not set, adding tops of rolls, cut-sides up, to baking sheet for the last 5 min.
7. After that, you sprinkle eggs with chives and replace tops of rolls.
8. Make sure you serve with remaining bacon slices.

Overnight Stuffed French toast

Ingredients:

6 tablespoons of sugar

8 eggs

2 cups of blueberries

2 tub (about 8 oz. each) PHILADELPHIA 1/3 Less Fat than Cream Cheese

16 slices of cinnamon-swirl bread

1 cup of milk

4 cups of sliced fresh strawberries

Directions:

1. First, you mix reduced-fat cream cheese and sugar until blended; spread onto bread.
2. After which you place 8 bread slices, cream cheese-sides up, in 8-inch square baking dish sprayed with cooking spray.
3. After that, you cover with remaining bread slices, cream cheese-sides down.
4. Then you whisk eggs and milk until blended; pour over bread. Cover; refrigerate overnight.
5. At this point, you heat oven to a temperature of 350°F.
6. Bake, uncovered, for about 30 to 35 min. or until center is set and top is lightly browned.
7. Finally, you serve topped with fruit.

Easiest Soufflé Ever

Ingredients:

6 eggs (separated)

One tub (about 8 oz.) PHILADELPHIA Chive and Onion Cream Cheese Spread

Directions:

1. First, you heat oven to a temperature of 375°F.
2. After which you beat egg whites in medium bowl with mixer on high speed until stiff peaks form.
3. After that, you beat cream cheese spread in large bowl with mixer until creamy.
4. Then you add egg yolks; beat until well blended.
5. This is when you gently stir in egg whites until well blended.
6. At this point, you pour into 1-1/2-qt. baking dish sprayed with cooking spray.
7. Finally, you bake for about 24 to 26 min. or until top is puffed and golden brown.

Walnut–Black Pepper Cookies
Ingredients:

6 tablespoons of cane sugar

Pinches of salt

2 cup (4 ounces each) raw walnuts (pounded or coarsely ground)

Granulated sugar for sprinkling the cookies

1 cup (about 2 sticks) soft unsalted butter

1 ½ teaspoons of freshly ground black pepper

6 tablespoons of semi-runny honey (preferably darker honey here, such as wildflower or chestnut)

2 cups of flour

Yield: 4 dozen cookies

Directions:

1. Meanwhile, you heat the oven to a temperature of 300°F.
2. After which you line a baking sheet with parchment paper.
3. After that, you cream the butter with the sugar until light and fluffy.
4. Then you add the black pepper, pinch of salt, and honey; mix to incorporate.
5. At this point, you add the nuts and flour, and mix with the electric mixer in a few minutes until the dough forms moist clumps.
6. This is when you roll large teaspoonful of the batter between your clean hands to make little balls.
7. Furthermore, you place the balls on the baking sheet, and press down on them twice with the tines of a fork to make a crosshatch pattern.
8. After that, you sprinkle with a little bit of granulated sugar.
9. Bake the cookies for about 25 minutes, or until their bottoms have turned golden-nutty brown and set aside to cool.
10. For a complete walnut experience, I suggest you enjoy the cookies with sip full of the following sweet walnut liquor.

Foil-Pack Chicken & Broccoli Dinner

Ingredients:

2-1 cups of water

8 cups of broccoli florets
1 cup of KRAFT Classic Ranch Dressing

2 pkg. (6 oz. each) STOVE TOP Stuffing Mix for Chicken

12 small boneless skinless chicken breasts (2-1 lb.), 1/2 inch thick

2-1 cups of KRAFT Shredded Cheddar Cheese

½ cup of OSCAR MAYER Real Bacon Bits

Directions:

1. First, you heat oven to a temperature of 400°F.
2. After which you combine stuffing mix and water; spoon onto centers of 12 large sheets heavy-duty foil.
3. After that, you top with remaining ingredients; fold to make 12 packets.
4. At this point, you place on rimmed baking sheet.
5. Then you bake 30 to 35 min. or until chicken is done (165°F).
6. This is when you remove packets from oven and let stand 5 minute.
7. Finally, you cut slits in foil to release steam before opening packets.

Crust less Bacon and Cheese Quiche

Ingredients:

2 tomato (chopped, divided)
2 cups of sliced fresh mushrooms

2/3 cup of BREAKSTONE'S Reduced Fat (or preferably KNUDSEN Light Sour Cream)

2 cups of KRAFT 2% Milk Shredded Mozzarella Cheese

10 green onions (chopped, divided)

24 slices of OSCAR MAYER Bacon

24 eggs

2 cups of KRAFT 2% Milk Shredded Cheddar Cheese

Directions:

1. First, you heat oven to a temperature of 350°F.
2. After which you reserve 4 tablespoons of each onions and tomatoes.
3. After that, you cook bacon in large skillet until crisp.
4. Then you remove bacon from skillet, reserving 2 Tablespoons of drippings in skillet.
5. At this point, you drain bacon on paper towels.
6. Furthermore, you add mushrooms to reserved drippings.
7. Cook and stir for about 2 min. or until tender.
8. This is when you remove from heat. Crumble bacon and add to skillet with remaining onions and tomatoes; mix well.
9. After that, you beat eggs and sour cream with whisk until blended.
10. Then you pour into 13x9-inch baking dish sprayed with cooking spray; top with bacon mixture and cheeses.
11. Bake for about 30 min. or until center is set.
12. Finally, you top with reserved onions and tomatoes and let stand for 5 min. before cutting to serve.

Sky-High Brunch Bake

Ingredients:

12 eggs (beaten)

Dash hot pepper sauce

8 slices cooked OSCAR MAYER Bacon (crumbled)
2 cups of chopped red peppers

2 pkg. (17.3 oz. each) frozen puff pastry (4 sheets), thawed

2 cups of POLLY-O Original Ricotta Cheese

4 pkg. (10 oz. each) frozen chopped spinach (thawed, well drained)

2-1 cups of KRAFT Shredded Cheddar Cheese

Directions:

1. First, you heat oven to a temperature of 400°F.
2. After which you unfold pastry sheets and roll out 1 sheet to 11-inch square; set aside.
3. After that, you roll out remaining sheet to 12-inch square; use to line bottom and side of 2 (9-inch) spring form pan sprayed with cooking spray.
4. Make sure you reserve 2 tablespoons of eggs.
5. At this point, you mix remaining eggs with ricotta, hot sauce and spinach.
6. Furthermore, you layer half each of the bacon, cheddar, ricotta mixture and peppers in crust. Repeat layers.
7. After which you cover with remaining pastry sheet; fold under edges of pastry, then tuck inside pan.
8. This is when you brush pastry with reserved egg and then cut slits in top crust.
9. Bake for approximately 45 to 55 min. or until golden brown.
10. Then you cool for about 10 min. run small knife around edge of pan to loosen crust before removing rim.

Easiest Soufflé Ever

Ingredients:

2 tub (8 oz. each) PHILADELPHIA Chive and Onion Cream Cheese Spread

12 eggs (separated)

Directions:

1. First, you heat oven to a temperature of 375°F.
2. After which you beat egg whites in medium bowl with mixer on high speed until stiff peaks form.
3. After that, you beat cream cheese spread in large bowl with mixer until creamy.
4. Then you add egg yolks; beat until well blended.
5. At this point, you gently stir in egg whites until well blended.
6. Furthermore, you pour into 2-1/2-qt. baking dish sprayed with cooking spray.
7. Then you bake for about 24 to 26 min. or until top is puffed and golden brown.

Overnight Stuffed French toast

Ingredients:

6 tablespoons of sugar

8 eggs

2 cups of blueberries

2 tub (8 oz. each) PHILADELPHIA 1/3 Less Fat than Cream Cheese

16 slices cinnamon-swirl bread

1 cup of milk

4 cups of sliced fresh strawberries

Directions:

1. First, you mix reduced-fat cream cheese and sugar until blended; spread onto bread.
2. After that, you place 8 bread slices, cream cheese-sides up, in 2 (8-inch) square baking dish sprayed with cooking spray.
3. After that, you cover with remaining bread slices, cream cheese-sides down.
4. Then you whisk eggs and milk until blended; pour over bread.
5. This is when you cover; refrigerate overnight.
6. Finally, you heat oven to a temperature of 350°F.
7. Bake, uncovered, for about 30 to 35 min. or until center is set and top is lightly browned.
8. Make sure you serve topped with fruit.

Cheesy Egg-in-a-Bowl

Ingredients:

12 slices of cooked OSCAR MAYER Bacon (divided)
1 Tablespoon of chopped fresh chives

6 dinner rolls (3-1/2 inch)

6 oz. of VELVEETA® (cut into 6 slices)

6 eggs

Directions:

1. First, you heat oven to a temperature of 375°F.
2. After which you cut tops off rolls; set aside.
3. After that, you make 1-inch-deep indentation in center of bottom half of each roll.
4. Then you crumble 6 bacon slices; sprinkle into bread bowls.
5. At this point, you top with VELVEETA and slip 1 cracked egg into each bowl; place on baking sheet.
6. Furthermore, you bake for about 20 to 25 min. or until egg whites are completely set and yolks begin to thicken but are not set, adding tops of rolls, cut-sides up, to baking sheet for the last 5 min.
7. Finally, you sprinkle eggs with chives and then replace tops of rolls.
8. Make sure you serve with remaining bacon slices.

Mixed Nut Waldorf salad

Ingredients:

1/3 cup of PLANTERS Lightly Salted Nutrition Heart Healthy Mix (coarsely chopped)

3 Tablespoons of KRAFT Light Mayo Reduced Fat Mayonnaise

3 apples (about 1 lb.), finely chopped

1/3 cup of celery (chopped)

Directions:

All you do is combine all ingredients.

Enjoy!

Bacon Spinach Salad

Ingredients:

2 cups of sliced fresh mushrooms

8 slices of cooked OSCAR MAYER Turkey Bacon (chopped)

1 cup of KRAFT Lite CATALINA Dressing

10 cups of loosely packed torn spinach leaves

1 cup of thin red onion wedges

4 hard-cooked eggs (chopped)

Direction:

1. First, you combine all ingredients except dressing in large bowl.
2. After which you add dressing just before serving.
3. Then you mix lightly.

Sunburst Fruit Salad

Ingredients:

2 Tablespoons of honey

1 cup of seedless red grapes
1 cup of fresh blueberries
3 cups of halved fresh strawberries

½ cup of BREAKSTONE'S (or preferably KNUDSEN Sour Cream)

¼ teaspoon of zest and 1 Tablespoon of juice from 1 lime

4 kiwis (peeled, sliced)

1-1/2 cups of fresh pineapple chunks (about 1 inch)

3 navel oranges (peeled, quartered and sliced)

Directions:

1. First, you mix sour cream, honey, zest and juice.
2. After which, you refrigerate until ready to use.
3. After that, you arrange fruit in circular pattern on round plate, starting at center of plate.
4. Then you serve with sour cream dressing.

Easy Caramel Sticky Buns

Ingredients:

4 Tablespoons of milk

2 cans (about 8 oz. each) refrigerated crescent dinner rolls

4 tablespoons of raisins

32 KRAFT Caramels

1 ½ cups of chopped PLANTERS Pecans (divided)

½ cups of sugar

2 teaspoons of ground cinnamon

Directions:

1. First, you heat oven to a temperature of 375°F.
2. After which you microwave caramels and milk in microwaveable bowl on HIGH 1-1/2 to 2 min. or until caramels are completely melted, stirring after each **minute**.
3. After that, you pour into 8-inch round pan sprayed with cooking spray; top with ½ cup nuts.
4. At this point, you unroll crescent roll dough; separate into 2 rectangles.
5. Then you press perforations in each rectangle together to seal.
6. Furthermore, you mix remaining nuts, sugar, cinnamon and raisins; sprinkle over dough.
7. After which you roll up each rectangle, jelly-roll fashion, starting at one short end; cut into 4 slices.
8. This is when you place, cut sides down, in prepared pan. (Note: feel free to sprinkle with any sugar mixture that may have fallen out of rolls.)
9. Bake for about 17 to 20 min. or until lightly browned
10. After that, you immediately invert pan onto plate; remove pan.
11. Finally, you spread any caramel from pan over buns. Cool slightly.

Chocolate Chip-Banana Bread

Ingredients:

1 ½ cups of sugar

1 ½ cups of BREAKSTONE'S (or preferably KNUDSEN Sour Cream)

2-1 cups of flour

1 teaspoon of baking soda

1 ½ cups of BAKER'S Semi-Sweet Chocolate Morsels

1/2 cup of butter (softened)

4 eggs

2 cups of mashed fully ripe bananas (about 6)

2-1 teaspoons of CALUMET Baking Powder

1 teaspoon of salt

Directions:

1. First, you heat oven to a temperature of 350°F.
2. After which you beat butter and sugar in large bowl with mixer until blended.
3. After that, you add eggs and sour cream; mix well.
4. Then you add bananas and combined dry ingredients; mix just until moistened.
5. This is when you stir in chocolate morsels.
6. At this point, you pour into greased and floured 8x4-inch loaf pan.
7. Bake for about 1 hour or until toothpick inserted in center comes out clean.
8. Furthermore, you cool for 5 min.; remove from pan to wire rack.
9. Finally, you cool completely before slicing and make sure you refrigerate leftovers.

Wild Berry-Oatmeal Cheesecake Muffins

Ingredients:

2 cups of buttermilk

½ cup of granulated sugar

2 cups of flour

2 teaspoons of CALUMET Baking Powder

1 teaspoon of salt

2 cups of fresh or frozen mixed berries (such as blackberries, blueberries and raspberries)

2 cups of old-fashioned or quick-cooking oats

2 pkg. (about 8 oz. each) PHILADELPHIA Cream Cheese, softened

6 tablespoons of orange zest

1 ½ cup of packed brown sugar

1 teaspoon of baking soda

2 eggs (beaten)

½ cup of butter (melted)

Directions:

1. First, you heat oven to a temperature of 350°F.
2. After which you combine oats and buttermilk in medium bowl; let stand 10 min.
3. In the meantime, you mix cream cheese, granulated sugar and orange zest until blended; set aside.
4. After that you combine flour, baking powder, brown sugar, baking soda and salt in large bowl.
5. Then you add egg and butter to oat mixture; mix well.
6. Furthermore, you add to flour mixture; stir just until moistened.

7. After which you gently stir in berries.
8. At this point, you spoon half the batter evenly into 36 paper-lined muffin cups; top with cream cheese mixture.
9. Then you cover with remaining batter.
10. Bake for about 23 to 25 min. or until toothpick inserted in centers comes out clean.
11. Finally, you cool in pan 10 minute and remove from pan to wire rack; cool completely.

Blintz Brunch Bake

Ingredients:

1 container (about 15 oz.) POLLY-O Natural Part Skim Ricotta Cheese

¾ cup of sugar (divided)

1 cup of flour

1 Tablespoon of CALUMET Baking Powder

2 pkg. (about 8 oz. each) PHILADELPHIA Neufchatel Cheese, softened

5 eggs (divided)

2 teaspoons of zest and 3 Tablespoons of juice from 1 lemon

¾ cup of butter or margarine (melted)

¼ cup of milk

Directions:

1. First, you heat oven to a temperature of 325°F.
2. After which you beat Neufchatel, 1/4 cup sugar, ricotta, 2 eggs, lemon zest and juice in large bowl with mixer until blended.
3. After that, you whisk remaining eggs, butter, sugar, flour, milk and baking powder in separate bowl until blended.
4. At this point, you spread 1/3 of the batter onto bottom of 13x9-inch baking dish sprayed with cooking spray; cover with Neufchatel mixture, then remaining batter.
5. Then you bake 45 min. or until center is set.

Creamy Lemon Squares

Ingredients:

½ cup of flour

¼ cup of cold margarine

1 cup of granulated sugar

2 Tablespoons of flour

¼ cup of fresh lemon juice

2 teaspoons of powdered sugar

20 reduced-fat vanilla wafers (finely crushed about ¾ cup)

¼ cup of packed brown sugar

1 pkg. (about 8 oz.) PHILADELPHIA Neufchatel Cheese (softened)

2 eggs

3 Tablespoons of lemon zest (divided)

¼ teaspoon of CALUMET Baking Powder

Directions:

1. First, you heat oven to a temperature of 350°F.
2. After which you line 8-inch square pan with Reynolds Wrap® Aluminum Foil.
3. After that, you mix first 3 ingredients in medium bowl.
4. Then you cut in margarine with pastry blender or 2 knives until mixture resembles coarse crumbs.
5. Press onto bottom of prepared pan and bake for about 15 minute.
6. At this point, you beat Neufchatel and granulated sugar with mixer until blended.
7. Furthermore, you add eggs and 2 Tablespoons of flour; mix well.
8. After that, you blend in 1 Tablespoon of zest, juice and baking powder; pour over crust.
9. Bake for about 25 to 28 minute or until center is set.
10. Cool completely and refrigerate for about 2 hours.

Delectable Camping Recipes

11. Finally, you sprinkle with powdered sugar and remaining zest just before serving.

DELECTABLE APPITIZER RECIPES

Chunky Vegetable Hummus Spread

Ingredients:

½ cup of chopped seeded cucumbers

1 plum tomato (chopped)

3 whole wheat pita breads (about 7 inch), torn into 8 pieces each

1 container (about 7 oz.) ATHENOS Original Hummus

¼ cup of finely chopped red onions

¼ cup of ATHENOS Traditional Crumbled Feta Cheese

Directions:

1. First, you spread hummus onto plate.
2. After which, you top with layers of all remaining ingredients except bread.
3. Then you serve with bread.

Plantain Chips with Jicama and Avocado Salsa

Ingredients:

1 cup of finely chopped red peppers

4 tablespoons of chopped fresh cilantro

2 small avocado (chopped)

4 tablespoons of KRAFT Grated Parmesan Cheese

4 cups of finely chopped jicama

2 jalapeño pepper, seeded (finely chopped)

½ cup of KRAFT Zesty Lime Vinaigrette Dressing

2 cups of oil

4 green plantains (each cut into 24 slices)

Directions:

1. First, you combine jicama, red peppers, jalapeño pepper, fresh cilantro and Lime Vinaigrette Dressing in medium bowl.
2. After which you gently stir in avocados.
3. After that, you heat oil in medium skillet on medium heat.
4. Then you add plantains; cook 3 min. or until tender and evenly browned, turning after 1-1/2 min.
5. At this point, you use slotted spoon to transfer plantains to work surface; flatten to 1/4-inch thickness.
6. This is when you return plantains, 6 at a time, to skillet; cook 1 min. on each side or until each is golden brown on both sides.
7. Furthermore, you remove from skillet; drain on paper towel-covered plate.
8. After that, you cover to keep warm.
9. Make sure you repeat with remaining plantains.
10. Finally, you sprinkle plantain chips with cheese.
11. Make sure you serve with salsa.

Mini Cheeseburger Appetizers

Ingredients:

½ cup of dry Italian-style bread crumbs

2 eggs

36 grape tomatoes

2 lb. of lean ground beef

2 clove garlic (minced)

9 oz. CRACKER BARREL Sharp Cheddar Cheese (cut into 36 slices)

Directions:

1. First, you heat grill to medium heat.
2. After which you mix lean ground beef, dry Italian-style bread crumbs, garlic and egg just until blended; shape into 36 (1-inch) balls.
3. After that, you flatten slightly to form patties.
4. At this point, you spray large sheet of foil with cooking spray; place on grill grate.
5. Then you add patties; grill for about 2 to 3 min. on each side or until done (160°F).
6. Finally, you thread 1 each burger, cheese slice and tomato onto each of 36 toothpicks.

Horseradish-Bacon Dip

Ingredients:

1 cups of BREAKSTONE'S Reduced Fat (or preferably KNUDSEN Light Sour Cream)

2 Tablespoons of KRAFT Horseradish Sauce

Thin wheat snack crackers

1-1/2 cups of KRAFT 2% Milk Shredded Sharp Cheddar Cheese

¼ cup of crumbled cooked OSCAR MAYER Bacon

2 Tablespoons of chopped fresh chives

Directions:

1. First, you blend cheese, sour cream, bacon and horseradish sauce in blender until well blended.
2. After which you transfer to bowl.
3. After that, you stir in chives and refrigerate for 1 hour.
4. Then you serve with crackers.

Lime-Marinated Shrimp & Cheddar Appetizers

Ingredients:

2 teaspoons of olive oil

2 small jalapeño pepper, seeded (finely chopped)

8 oz. CRACKER BARREL Vermont Sharp-White Cheddar Cheese (cut into 32 slices)

8 grape tomatoes (quartered)

16 frozen uncooked cleaned medium shrimp (1/2 lb.), thawed

4 tablespoons of fresh lime juice

32 gluten-free blue tortilla chips (about 3 oz.)

2/3 cup of guacamole

Directions:

1. First, you heat grill to medium-high heat.
2. After which you thread shrimp onto skewers; brush with oil.
3. After that, you grill for about 2 to 4 min. or until shrimp turn pink, turning once.
4. Then you remove shrimp from skewers; cut lengthwise in half.
5. At this point, you place in medium bowl and add lime juice and peppers; mix lightly.
6. Finally, you top chips with shrimp mixture, cheese, guacamole and tomatoes.

Easy Deviled Eggs

Ingredients:

½ cup of MIRACLE WHIP Dressing

½ teaspoon of paprika

24 hard-cooked eggs

½ cup of GREY POUPON Dijon Mustard

Directions:

1. First, you cut eggs lengthwise in half.
2. After which you remove yolks; place in small bowl.
3. After that, you add dressing and mustard; mix well.
4. Finally, you spoon into egg white halves; sprinkle with paprika.

MIRACLE WHIP Creamy Spinach & Artichoke Dip

Ingredients:

1 cup of BREAKSTONE'S Reduced Fat (or preferably KNUDSEN Light Sour Cream)

1 pkg. (about 9 oz.) frozen chopped spinach, cooked, cooled and well drained

3 canned chipotle peppers in adobo sauce (chopped)

1 cup of MIRACLE WHIP Dressing

1 can (about 14 oz.) artichoke hearts (drained, finely chopped)

½ teaspoon of garlic powder

3 green onions (thinly sliced)

Direction:

1. First you combine the entire ingredients.
2. Then you refrigerate for 1 hour or until chilled.

Basil & Tomato-Feta Bruschetta

Ingredients:

4 tablespoons of oil (divided)

2 pkg. (4 oz. each) ATHENOS Traditional Crumbled Feta Cheese

4 tablespoons of chopped basil

½ teaspoon of pepper

2 French bread baguette (16 oz. each), cut into slices

14 plum tomatoes, chopped (about 5 cups)

1 cup of finely chopped red onions

2 tablespoons of chopped black olives

Directions:

1. First, you heat broiler.
2. After which you broil bread slices for about 2 to 3 min. on each side or until lightly toasted on both sides.
3. After that, you brush evenly with 1 Tablespoon of oil.
4. Then you combine remaining ingredients with remaining oil.
5. Finally, you spoon onto toast slices just before serving.

Delectable Camping Recipes

Cheesy Spinach and Bacon Dip

Ingredients:

1 lb. (about 16 oz.) VELVEETA (cut into 1/2-inch cubes)

8 slices of cooked OSCAR MAYER Bacon (crumbled)

1 pkg. (about 10 oz. each) frozen chopped spinach (thawed, drained)

4 oz. (about 1/2 of 8-oz. pkg.) PHILADELPHIA Cream Cheese, cubed

1 can (about 10 oz.) RO*TEL Diced Tomatoes and Green Chilies (undrained)

Directions:

1. First, you microwave ingredients in microwaveable bowl on HIGH 5 min. or until VELVEETA is completely melted and mixture is well blended.
2. After that you keep stirring after 3 min.

Kielbasa Bites with Creamy Mustard Dipping Sauce

Ingredients:

6 KRAFT Singles

2 Tablespoons of poppy seed

¼ cup of BREAKSTONE'S or KNUDSEN Sour Cream

1 Tablespoons of chopped fresh parsley

1 can (about 11 oz.) of refrigerated thin crust pizza dough

1 pkg. (about 14 oz.) of OSCAR MAYER Turkey Polka Kielbasa

¼ cup of KRAFT Real Mayo Mayonnaise

2 Tablespoons of GREY POUPON Dijon Mustard

Directions:

1. First, you heat oven to a temperature of 400°F.
2. After which you remove pizza dough from can. (Do not unroll dough.)
3. After that, you place dough on work surface; cut crosswise in half.
4. Then you enroll each half and place 3 Singles down center of each dough piece; top diagonally with 1 sausage link.
5. At this point, you fold corners of dough over ends of each sausage link, then fold 1 of the remaining corners of dough over sausage.
6. This is when you roll dough to completely enclose sausage; pinch seams together to seal.
7. Furthermore, you spray lightly with cooking spray; roll in poppy seed until evenly coated.
8. After that, you place, seam sides down, on baking sheet sprayed with cooking spray.
9. Bake for about 12 min. or until golden brown.
10. In the meantime, you mix remaining ingredients until blended.
11. Finally, you cut each log into 14 slices.
12. Make sure you serve with sauce.

Rattlesnake Bite Hot Dog Appetizers

Ingredients:

2 can (about 16.3 oz. each) large refrigerated flaky biscuits (16 biscuits)

2 pkg. (about 16 oz. each) OSCAR MAYER Jalapeño Dogs

Directions:

1. First, you heat oven to a temperature of 375°F.
2. After which you pat hot dogs dry with paper towel and separate biscuits.
3. After that, you cut each hot dog and biscuit into quarters; press biscuits to flatten slightly.
4. Then you place 1 hot dog piece on center of each biscuit piece and bring 2 opposite corners of biscuit over hot dog, then press points together to seal.
5. At this point, you arrange 32 wrapped hot dog pieces in "s" shape on baking sheet to resemble snake, leaving no spaces between pieces.
6. Make sure you repeat on second baking sheet with remaining wrapped hot dog pieces.
7. Finally, you bake for about 15 min. or until golden brown.

Bacon Appetizer Crescents

16 slices OSCAR MAYER Bacon (cooked, crumbled)

½ cup of finely chopped onions

4 cans (8 oz. each) refrigerated crescent dinner rolls

2 pkg. (8 oz. each) PHILADELPHIA Cream Cheese, softened

2/3 cup of KRAFT Grated Parmesan Cheese

4 tablespoons of chopped fresh parsley

2 tablespoons of milk

Directions:

1. First, you heat oven to a temperature of 375°F.
2. After which you mix all ingredients except crescent dough.
3. After that, you separate each can of dough into 8 triangles; cut each triangle lengthwise in half.
4. Then you spread each dough triangle with 1 generous teaspoon cream cheese mixture; roll up, starting at short side of triangle.
5. Furthermore, you place, point-sides down, on baking sheet.
6. Finally, you bake for about 12 to 15 min. or until golden brown.
7. Make sure you serve warm.

DELECTABLE CHICKEN RECIPES

Sweet Heat Grilled Chicken Sandwich

Ingredients:

4 KRAFT Big Slice Hot Habanero Cheese Slices

¼ cup of KRAFT Real Mayo Mayonnaise

1 tomato (cut into 4 slices)

4 small boneless skinless chicken breasts (about 1 lb.)

4 pretzel sandwich rolls (split)

2 Tablespoons of mango chutney

½ cup of spring lettuce mix

Directions:

1. First, you heat grill to medium-high heat.
2. After which you grill chicken for about 6 to 8 minute on each side or until done (165°F).
3. After that, you top with cheese and add rolls, cut sides down, to grill for the last minute.
4. At this point, you mix mayo and chutney until blended; spread onto bottom halves of rolls.
5. Then you fill with chicken, lettuce and tomatoes.

Grilled Chicken Quesadillas

Ingredients:

2/3 cup of white vinegar

2 lb. boneless skinless chicken breasts (pounded to 1/2-inch thickness)
8 flour tortillas

½ cup of chopped fresh cilantro

2 red onion (sliced)

2 tablespoons of sugar

½ cup of KRAFT Original Barbecue Sauce

8 KRAFT Singles

Directions:

1. First, you heat grill to medium heat.
2. After which you cook onions in boiling water 5 min. or until tender; drain.
3. After that, you place onions in medium bowl and add vinegar and sugar; mix well.
4. Then you refrigerate until ready to use.
5. Furthermore, you grill chicken for about 5 to 6 min. on each side or until done (165°F), brushing with barbecue sauce for the last 5 min.
6. This is when you cut into thin strips.
7. In addition, you top tortillas with chicken, onions and Singles; fold in half.
8. After which you grill for about 1 to 2 min. on each side or until Singles are melted and quesadillas are lightly browned on both sides.
9. Finally, you sprinkle with cilantro.

Beer Can-Barbecue Chicken

Ingredients:

2 teaspoons of onion powder

1 teaspoons of black pepper

2 whole chicken (about 4 lb.)
1 cup of KRAFT Sweet Honey Barbecue Sauce

2 teaspoons of garlic powder

½ teaspoon of dried thyme leaves

2 can (about 24 oz.) beer

Directions:

1. First, you heat grill for indirect grilling: Light one side of grill, leaving other side unlit.
2. After which you close lid and heat grill to 375°F.
3. After that, you mix the onion powder, black pepper, garlic powder, paprika and dried thyme leaves rub onto chicken.
4. At this point, you open beer can; discard half the beer.
5. Then you place can on work surface; lower chicken over can, inserting can into tail end of chicken.
6. This is when you stand chicken on grate over unlit area, using the legs to help the chicken stand upright and then cover (Note: Can should remain in chicken on grill.)
7. Furthermore, you grill chicken for 1 hour; brush with ½ cup sauce.
8. After which you grill, uncovered, 15 min. or until chicken is done (165°F), monitoring for consistent grill temperature and brushing chicken frequently with remaining sauce.
9. After that, you remove from grill; cover loosely with foil.
10. Then you let stand for about 10 min. before removing chicken from can and carving chicken.
11. Finally, you discard any beer remaining in can.

Grilled White Chicken Pizza

Ingredients:

8 cloves garlic (minced)

2 ready-to-use thin baked pizza crust (about 12 inch each)

1 ½ cups of POLLY-O Natural Part Skim Ricotta Cheese

2 cups of KRAFT Shredded Mozzarella Cheese with a TOUCH OF PHILADELPHIA

4 tablespoons of coarsely chopped fresh basil leaves

2/3 cup of KRAFT Zesty Italian Dressing

4 small boneless skinless chicken breasts (1 lb.)

1 cup of KRAFT Shredded Parmesan Cheese

2/3 cup of chopped red bell peppers

½ teaspoon of black pepper

Directions:

1. First, you heat grill for indirect grilling:
2. After which you light one side of grill, leaving other side unlit.
3. After that, you close lid and heat grill to 400°F.
4. Then you mix dressing and garlic.
5. At this point, you drizzle 6 tablespoons over chicken in shallow dish; turn to evenly coat both sides of breasts.
6. Furthermore, you refrigerate for 5 min.
7. After which you place chicken over lit area of grill and then cook for about 6 to 8 min. on each side or until done (165°F).
8. This is when you cool slightly; cut into bite-size pieces.
9. In addition, you brush pizza crust with remaining dressing mixture; top with all remaining ingredients except basil.
10. At this point, you place pizza on grill over unlit area; cover.
11. Finally, you grill 12 to 15 min. or until cheese is melted and crust is golden brown, monitoring for consistent grill temperature.
12. Make sure you sprinkle with basil.

Grilled "Cola-Q" Chicken

Ingredients:

1 cup of KRAFT Original Barbecue Sauce

2 whole broiler-fryer chicken (6 lb.)

2 cups of cola

4 tablespoons of hot pepper sauce

Directions:

1. First, you heat grill for indirect grilling: Light one side of grill, leaving other side unlit.
2. After which you close lid and heat grill to 350°F.
3. In the meantime, you cook cola and barbecue sauce in saucepan on medium heat for 10 min., stirring occasionally.
4. After that, you remove from heat; stir in hot sauce and reserve 1 ½ cups of sauce to serve with the grilled chicken.
5. Then you cut out back bone of chicken carefully with kitchen shears or sharp knife.
6. At this point, you place chicken, skin side up, on work surface; press firmly to flatten.
7. Furthermore, you place chicken, breast side down, on grill grate over lit area; cover with lid.
8. After that, you grill 15 min.; turn, then place over unlit area and then grill for about 25 to 30 min. or until chicken is done (165°F).
9. This is when you keep monitoring for consistent grill temperature, turning and brushing occasionally with remaining barbecue sauce mixture for the last 15 min.
10. Finally, you serve with the reserved barbecue sauce mixture.

Grilled Chicken Flatbread

Ingredients:

1 tub (about 8 oz.) PHILADELPHIA 1/3 Less Fat than Cream Cheese

½ teaspoon of garlic powder
½ cup of roasted red pepper strips

1 cup of KRAFT Shredded Mozzarella Cheese

2 Tablespoons of sliced fresh basil

1 lb. of frozen pizza dough (thawed)

2 Tablespoons of milk

1 boneless skinless chicken breast (about 6 oz.), grilled, and sliced

1 cup of sliced drained canned artichoke hearts

2 Tablespoons of KRAFT Grated Parmesan Cheese

Directions:

1. First, you heat oven to a temperature of 425°F.
2. After which you pat pizza dough into 16x12-inch rectangle on lightly floured baking sheet and bake for 10 min.
3. After that, you mix reduced-fat cream cheese, milk and garlic powder until blended; spread onto pizza crust.
4. Then you top with chicken, peppers, artichokes and cheeses.
5. Finally, you bake for 10 to 12 min. or until mozzarella is melted and edge of crust is golden brown.
6. Then you top with basil.

Cheesy Chicken & Veggie Mac

Ingredients:

2 pkg. (about 20 oz.) frozen mixed vegetables (such as carrots, broccoli, cauliflower)

½ cup of vegetable oil spread

¼ teaspoon of garlic powder

2 pkg. (14 ½ oz.) KRAFT Macaroni and Cheese Dinner

½ cup of milk

1 lb. of boneless skinless chicken breasts, cooked, chopped (about 2 cups)

Directions:

1. First, you cook Macaroni in large saucepan as directed on package, adding vegetables to the boiling water with the macaroni.
2. After which you drain; return to pan.
3. After that, you add Cheese Sauce Mix and remaining ingredients; mix well.
4. Then you cook on low heat for about 1 to 2 min. or until heated through, stirring occasionally.

Butterflied Chicken, Beans & Corn Salad

Ingredients:

8 small boneless skinless chicken breasts (about 2 lb.), butterflied

3 Tablespoons of fresh lime juice

1 can (about 15 oz.) chickpeas (garbanzo beans), rinsed

1 small onion (cut lengthwise in half, then crosswise into thin slices)

1/3 cup of chopped fresh cilantro

1 pkg. (about 5 oz.) spring lettuce mix

6 slices of OSCAR MAYER Bacon (chopped)

½ cup of KRAFT Zesty Italian Dressing

1 can (about 15.5 oz.) red kidney beans (rinsed)

1 pkg. (about 10 oz.) frozen corn (thawed)

1 small jalapeño pepper (thinly sliced)

1 avocado (chopped, divided)

Directions:

1. First, you cook and stir bacon in large skillet on medium heat until crisp.
2. After which you remove bacon from skillet with slotted spoon; drain on paper towels.
3. After that, you drain and wipe out skillet with paper towels.
4. Then you add 4 chicken breasts to skillet; cook 2 min., turning once.
5. At this point, you cover and cook 5 min. or until done (165°F).
6. Furthermore, you remove from skillet; set aside.
7. This you repeat with remaining chicken.
8. After that, you mix dressing and lime juice until blended.
9. In addition, you combine beans, peppers, corn, onions, cilantro, bacon and half the avocados in large bowl.
10. After which you add ½ cup dressing mixture; toss to coat.
11. Finally, you toss lettuce with remaining dressing mixture.
12. Then you top with chicken, bean mixture and remaining avocados.

Sweet BBQ Chicken Kabobs

Ingredients:

4 cups of fresh pineapple chunks

6 tablespoons of frozen orange juice concentrate (thawed)

2 lb. of boneless skinless chicken breasts (cut into 1-1/2-inch pieces)

2 each red and green pepper (cut into 1-1/2-inch pieces)

1 cup of KRAFT Original Barbecue Sauce

Directions:

1. First, you heat grill to medium-high heat.
2. After which you thread chicken alternately with pineapple and peppers onto 16 long wooden skewers, using 2 skewers placed side-by-side for each kabob.
3. After that, you mix barbecue sauce and juice concentrate; brush half evenly onto kabobs.
4. Then you grill 8 to 10 min. or until chicken is done, turning and brushing occasionally with remaining sauce.

DELECTABLE BBQ PORK CHOP AND PORK CHOP RECIPES

Barbecue Pork Chops with Mango Salsa

Ingredients:

1 cup of KRAFT Sweet Brown Sugar Barbecue Sauce

½ cup of finely chopped red onions

4 tablespoons of KRAFT Zesty Lime Vinaigrette Dressing

8 bone-in pork loin center chops (about 3lb.), 1/2 inch thick

2 mango (finely chopped)

2 jalapeño pepper (seeded, finely chopped)

Directions:

1. First, you heat grill to medium heat.
2. After which you grill chops for 4 min. on each side.
3. After that, you brush with barbecue sauce and grill for about 3 to 5 min. or until done (145°F), turning and brushing occasionally with remaining barbecue sauce.
4. Then you remove chops from grill and let stand for 3 min.
5. In the meantime, you combine remaining ingredients.
6. Finally, you serve chops topped with mango mixture.

Classic BBQ Pork Chops

Ingredients:

4 tablespoons of plus 4 teaspoons of sugar (divided)

8 bone-in pork chops (3 lb.), 1/2 inch thick

4 teaspoons of onion powder

1 cup of KRAFT Original (or preferably Thick and Spicy Barbecue Sauce)

4 cups of water

4 tablespoons of kosher salt

2 tablespoons of paprika

1 teaspoon of ground black pepper

Directions:

1. First, you mix water, 4 tablespoons of sugar and salt until sugar and salt are dissolved.
2. After that, you pour over chops in reseal able plastic bag.
3. After which, you seal bag; turn to evenly coat chops with brine.
4. Then you refrigerate for 1 hour.
5. In the meantime, you mix remaining sugar and seasonings.
6. Furthermore, you heat grill to medium-high heat.
7. After that, you remove chops from brine; discard bag and brine.
8. At this point, you coat chops evenly with seasoning mixture.
9. Finally, you grill 5 to 6 min. on each side or until done (145°F), brushing with barbecue sauce for the last few minutes.
10. Then you remove from grill and let stand for 3 min.

BBQ "Porkwich"

Ingredients:

2 teaspoons of black pepper

1 cup of KRAFT Original Barbecue Sauce

12 KRAFT Singles

4 cups of baby spinach leaves

12 boneless pork chops (3 lb.), 1/2 inch thick

2 tablespoons of oil (divided)

12 Kaiser Rolls (split, toasted)

2 tomatoes (cut into 6 slices)

Directions:

1. First, you round chops to 1/4-inch thickness.
2. After which you sprinkle both sides of chops with pepper.
3. After that, you heat half the oil in large skillet on medium heat.
4. Then you add 3 chops; cook for 3 min. or until done (145° F), turning after 1-1/2 min.
5. This is when you remove from skillet; cover to keep warm.
6. Furthermore, you repeat with remaining oil and chops.
7. At this point, you return chops to skillet and add barbecue sauce.
8. After which you cook for 2 min. or until chops are completely covered with sauce and sauce is heated through.
9. Finally, you fill rolls with chops and remaining ingredients.

BBQ Smoked Pork Chops with Jicama Mixed Salad

Ingredients:

2 Tablespoons of chopped chipotle peppers in adobo sauce (divided)

½ cup of KRAFT Original Barbecue Sauce

½ small head cabbage (quartered)

4 carrots (about 1/2 lb.), shredded

½ cup of KRAFT Real Mayo Mayonnaise

2 Tablespoons of lime juice

6 smoked bone-in pork chops (about 2-1/2 lb.), 1/2 inch thick

2 small jicama (cut into match like sticks)

Directions:

1. First, you heat grill to medium heat.
2. After which you mix mayo, 2 tablespoons of peppers and lime juice; set aside.
3. After that, you mix remaining peppers with barbecue sauce.
4. Then you brush chops with half the barbecue sauce mixture.
5. At this point, you grill chops with cabbage 4 min. or until heated through (160°F), turning chops and brushing with remaining barbecue sauce mixture after 2 min.
6. This is when you remove chops from grill; turn cabbage.
7. Furthermore, you continue to grill cabbage 4 min.
8. After that, you shred or thinly slice cabbage; place in large bowl.
9. Finally, you add jicama, carrots and mayo mixture; toss to coat.
10. Make sure you serve with the chops.

Zesty Pork Chops and Grilled Vegetables

Ingredients:

½ cup of KRAFT Lite Zesty Italian Dressing

4 zucchini (cut diagonally into 1/4-inch-thick slices)

8 bone-in pork chops, 1/2 inch thick (2 ½ lb.)

2 tablespoons of GREY POUPON Dijon Mustard

4 red peppers (cut lengthwise into wedges)

Directions:

1. Meanwhile, you heat grill to medium heat.
2. After which you pierce both sides of chops several times with fork; place in shallow dish.
3. After that, you combine dressing and mustard.
4. Then you pour half of the dressing mixture over chops; cover dish.
5. This is when you refrigerate at least 15 min. to marinate.
6. Furthermore, you set remaining dressing mixture aside for later use.
7. After that, you remove chops from marinade; discard marinade.
8. At this point, you grill chops and vegetables 7 to 8 min. on each side or until chops are cooked through (160°F) and vegetables are crisp-tender, brushing occasionally with the reserved dressing mixture.

Saucy Barbecued Pork Chop Skillet

Ingredients:

2 teaspoons of oil

1 cup of KRAFT Sweet Honey Barbecue Sauce

8 center-cut bone-in pork chops (2 lb.)

2 onions (sliced)

2 green pepper (cut into strips)

Directions:

first, you cook chops in hot oil in large nonstick skillet on medium heat 5 min. on each side or until browned on both sides.

1. After which you remove from skillet; cover to keep warm.
2. After that, you add vegetables to skillet; cook and stir 5 min.
3. Then you add barbecue sauce; stir and bring to boil.
4. At this point, you return chops to skillet; spoon sauce in skillet over chops.
5. Furthermore, you simmer for about 3 to 5 min. or until chops are done (145°F), turning after 3 min.
6. Finally, you serve chops topped with the vegetable mixture.

Cilantro-BBQ Grilled Pork Chops

Ingredients:

1 cup of chopped fresh cilantro

8 bone-in pork chops (about 3 lb.), 1/2 inch thick

1 cup of KRAFT Honey Spiced Pork Chop Barbecue Sauce

2 jalapeño pepper (seeded, finely chopped)

1 teaspoon of zest and 4 tablespoons of juice from 2 orange

Directions:

1. First, you heat grill to medium-high heat.
2. After which you mix all ingredients except chops.
3. After that, you reserve half for serving with the cooked chops.
4. Then you grill chops for 5 to 7 min. on each side or until done (145°F), brushing occasionally with remaining sauce.
5. Finally, you remove from grill; cover and let stand for 3 min.
6. Make sure you serve with reserved sauce.

BBQ Pork Wraps

Ingredients:

2 lb. boneless pork chops (cut into strips)

2 each green and red pepper (cut into strips)
16 flour tortillas (6 inch)

4 teaspoons of oil

2 onion (sliced)

1 cup of KRAFT Original Barbecue Sauce

Directions:

1. First, you heat oil in large nonstick skillet on medium-high heat.
2. After which you add meat; cook and stir for 2 to 3 min. or until evenly browned.
3. After that, you add vegetables; cook and stir for 2 to 3 min. or until meat is done and peppers are crisp-tender.
4. Then you stir in barbecue sauce; simmer on medium-low heat for 6 to 8 min. or until heated through, stirring occasionally.
5. Finally, you spoon meat mixture down centers of tortillas; roll up.

Quick BBQ Pork Sandwiches

Ingredients:

8 boneless pork chops (2 lb.)
8 Kaiser rolls (split)
2 large tomato (cut into 4 slices)

2 cups of KRAFT Original Barbecue Sauce (divided)

8 slices of onion

8 lettuce leaves

Directions:

1. First, you heat grill to medium heat.
2. After which you reserve ½ cup barbecue sauce for spreading onto rolls; set aside.
3. After that, you place chops on grill; brush lightly with some of the remaining barbecue sauce.
4. Then you grill for 6 to 8 min. on each side or until done (160°F), brushing occasionally with remaining barbecue sauce and adding onions to the grill for the last 4 min., turning after 2 min.
5. Finally, you spread rolls with reserved sauce; fill with chops, onions, lettuce and tomatoes.

Pork Chops with Fully Loaded Smashed Potatoes

Ingredients:

6 slices of OSCAR MAYER Bacon (chopped)

¾ cup of fat-free reduced-sodium chicken broth

1 cup of KRAFT Shredded Sharp Cheddar Cheese

1-1/2 lb. of small red potatoes (about 8), quartered

6 thin-cut bone-in pork chops (about 2 lb.), 1/2 inch thick

4 oz. (about 1/2 of 8-oz. pkg.) PHILADELPHIA Cream Cheese, cubed

3 Tablespoons of chopped fresh chives, divided

Directions:

1. First, you cook potatoes in boiling water in large saucepan for 20 to 25 min. or until tender.
2. In the meantime, you cook and stir bacon in large skillet on medium heat until crisp.
3. After which you remove bacon from skillet with slotted spoon; drain on paper towels.
4. After that, you discard all but 1 Tablespoon of drippings from skillet.
5. At this point, you add chops to drippings in skillet; cook on medium-high heat 3 min. on each side or until done (145°F).
6. Then you transfer chops to plate, reserving drippings in skillet; cover chops to keep warm.
7. Furthermore, you add broth to skillet; stir to scrape up browned bits from bottom of skillet.
8. This is when you add cream cheese; cook for 2 to 3 min. or until cream cheese is melted and sauce is thickened, stirring constantly with whisk.
9. In addition, you stir in 1 Tablespoon of chives.
10. After that, you drain potatoes; return to pan.
11. Then you mash to desired consistency.
12. Finally, you stir in cheddar, bacon and remaining chives.
13. Finally, you serve with meat and pan gravy.

Bruschetta Pork Chops

Ingredients:

1/4 pkt. (2 Tbsp.) SHAKE 'N BAKE Original Pork Seasoned Coating Mix

1/4 cup KRAFT Sun Dried Tomato Vinaigrette Dressing

2 butterflied boneless pork chops (1/2 lb.)

1 large plum tomato, chopped

1/2 cup KRAFT Shredded Low-Moisture Part-Skim Mozzarella Cheese

Directions:

1. First, you heat oven to a temperature of 425°F.
2. After which you coat chops with coating mix as directed on package.
3. After that, you place on baking sheet sprayed with cooking spray.
4. Then you bake for 20 min. or until chops are done (160°F).
5. In the meantime, you combine tomatoes and dressing.
6. This is when you top chops with tomato mixture and cheese.
7. Finally, you bake for 5 min. or until cheese is melted.

Five-Pepper Pork Chop Skillet

Ingredients:

2 teaspoons of ground black pepper

1 cup of fat-free reduced-sodium chicken broth

½ teaspoon of crushed red pepper

12 bone-in pork chops (about 4 lb.), 1/2 inch thick

2 each green, red and yellow bell pepper (coarsely chopped)

8oz. PHILADELPHIA Cream Cheese (cubed)

Directions:

1. First, you sprinkle chops with black pepper.
2. After which you add 3 chops to large nonstick skillet; cook on medium heat for 3 to 4 min. on each side or until done (145°F).
3. After that, you transfer to platter; cover to keep warm.
4. This you repeat with remaining chops.
5. Then you add bell peppers and broth to skillet; cook on medium-high heat 5 min. or until peppers are crisp-tender.
6. Furthermore, you stir in cream cheese and crushed pepper; cook and stir 2 to 3 min. or until sauce is blended and heated through.
7. Finally, you serve sauce over chops.

Smothered Pork Chops
Ingredients:

2 pkt. SHAKE 'N BAKE Original Pork Seasoned Coating Mix

2 jar (about 24 oz.) pork gravy

12 bone-in pork chops (10 oz. each), 1/2 inch thick

4 large onions (sliced)

2 tablespoons of oil

Directions:

1. First, you heat oven to a temperature of 375°F.
2. After which you coat chops with coating mix as directed on package; place in 13x9-inch pan.
3. After that, you toss onions with oil; place over chops.
4. Bake for 30 min.
5. Then you top with gravy; cover.
6. Finally, you bake for 15 min. or until chops are done (160°F).

Pork Chop Stuffing Bake

Ingredients:

6 boneless pork chops (about 1-1/2 lb.)

1 large onion (chopped)

½ cup of KRAFT Shredded Cheddar Cheese

1 pkg. (about 6 oz.) STOVE TOP Stuffing Mix for Chicken

1 can (about 10-3/4 oz.) condensed cream of mushroom soup

½ teaspoon of dried thyme leaves

Directions:

1. First, you heat oven to a temperature of 350°F.
2. After which you prepare stuffing as directed on package.
3. In the meantime, you cook chops in large ovenproof nonstick skillet on medium-high heat 4 min. on each side or until browned on both sides.
4. After that, you mix soup, onions and thyme; spoon over chops.
5. Then you top chops with stuffing; sprinkle with cheese.
6. Bake for about 20 to 25 min. or until chops are done (145°F).
7. Finally, you let stand for 3 min. before serving.

French Onion-Pork Chop Skillet

Ingredients:

2 onions (thinly sliced)

1 pkg. (about 6 oz.) STOVE TOP Stuffing Mix for Chicken

1 cup of KRAFT Shredded Low-Moisture Part-Skim Mozzarella Cheese

6 boneless pork chops (about 1-1/2 lb.), 1/2 inch thick

2 Tablespoons of Worcestershire sauce

1-1/2 cups of hot water

DIRECTIONS:

1. First, you cook chops and onions in large nonstick skillet on medium-high heat for 8 min., turning chops and stirring onions after 4 min. (Chops will not be done.)
2. After which, you remove chops from skillet.
3. After that, you cook onions additional 5 min. or until golden brown, stirring frequently.
4. Then you stir in Worcestershire sauce.
5. Furthermore, you return chops to skillet; spoon onion mixture over chops.
6. At this point, you combine stuffing mix and water; spoon around edge of skillet.
7. This is when you top chops and stuffing with cheese; cover.
8. Then you cook for 5 min. or until cheese is melted and chops are done (145°F).
9. Finally, you remove from heat and let stand for 3 min. before serving.

30-Minute Italian Pork Chop Dinner

Ingredients:

4 lean bone-in pork chops (about 1-1/2 lb.), 1/2 inch thick

1 each green and red pepper (cut into strips)

½ cup of KRAFT 2% Milk Shredded Mozzarella Cheese

2 cups of instant brown rice (uncooked)

1 teaspoon of dried oregano leaves (crushed)

¼ cup of KRAFT Lite Zesty Italian Dressing

1 can (about 14-1/2 oz.) Italian-style diced tomatoes (undrained)

Directions:

1. First, you cook rice as directed on package, omitting salt.
2. In the meantime, you cook chops in large nonstick skillet on high heat 2 min. or until bottoms of chops are browned; turn.
3. After that, you sprinkle with oregano; top with peppers, dressing and tomatoes.
4. Then you bring to boil on medium heat; simmer on low heat for 10 min. or until chops are done (145°F).
5. This is when you remove chops from skillet; cover to keep warm.
6. At this point, you cook vegetable mixture on high heat for 1 to 2 min. or until vegetables are tender and sauce is thickened, stirring occasionally.
7. Furthermore, you spoon rice onto serving plates; top with chops.
8. Finally, you spoon vegetable mixture over chops; sprinkle with cheese.

DELECTABLE DESSERT RECIPES

Rustic Chocolate-Cinnamon Bread Pudding

Ingredients:

½ cup of packed brown sugar

½ teaspoon of ground cinnamon

2 oz. of BAKER'S Semi-Sweet Chocolate (coarsely chopped)

½ cup (1/2 of 8-oz. tub) of PHILADELPHIA 1/3 Less Fat than Cream Cheese

2 egg whites

1-3/4 cups of fat-free milk

6 cups of cubed whole wheat bread (about 6 to 8 slices)

Directions:

1. First, you heat oven to a temperature of 350°F.
2. After which you beat reduced-fat cream cheese and sugar in large bowl with mixer until well blended.
3. After that, you add egg whites and cinnamon; mix well.
4. Then you gradually beat in milk until well blended.
5. At this point, you place bread in 8-inch square baking dish; top with chocolate and cream cheese mixture.
6. Finally, you bake for about 30 to 35 min. or until center is set. Cool slightly.

Quick Pear & Cranberry Crisp

Ingredients:

1 cup of dried cranberries

4 tablespoons of water

½ cup of old-fashioned (or preferably quick-cooking oats)

4 tablespoons of butter (melted)

8 pears (peeled, sliced)

2 pkg. (about 3 oz. each) JELL-O Lemon Flavor Gelatin

1 cup of crushed pecan shortbread cookies

½ cup of chopped PLANTERS Pecans

Directions:

1. First, you combine fruit in large bowl.
2. After which you add dry gelatin mix and water; toss to evenly coat fruit.
3. After that, you spoon into 8-inch-square microwaveable dish.
4. This is when you mix remaining ingredients; sprinkle over fruit mixture.
5. Furthermore, you microwave on HIGH for about 16 to 18 min. or until streusel topping is lightly browned, and fruit mixture is hot and bubbly.
6. Then you cool slightly.

Apple Crumble

Ingredients:

64 vanilla wafers (about 2-2/3 cups), coarsely crushed

4 teaspoons of ground cinnamon

1 tub (about 8 oz.) PHILADELPHIA Honey Pecan Cream Cheese Spread

8 small apples (about 2 lb.), peeled, chopped

¼ cup of sugar

Directions:

1. First, you heat oven to a temperature of 400°F.
2. After which you mix cream cheese spread and wafer crumbs with fork until mixture resembles coarse crumbs. (Do not overmix.)
3. After that, you toss apples with sugar and cinnamon; spoon into 1-1/2-qt. casserole.
4. At this point, you sprinkle with crumb mixture.
5. Then you bake for about 15 to 20 min. or until topping is lightly browned and apples are tender.
6. Finally, you serve warm and refrigerate leftovers.

PHILADELPHIA-Cherry Danish Dessert

Ingredients:

2 pkg. (about 8 oz. each) PHILADELPHIA Cream Cheese (softened)

1 egg white

3 Tablespoons of milk

2 cans (about 8 oz. each) refrigerated crescent dinner rolls (divided)

1-1/2 cups of powdered sugar (divided)

1 teaspoon of vanilla

1 can (about 20 oz.) cherry pie filling

Directions:

1. First, you heat oven to a temperature of 350°F.
2. After which you unroll 1 can crescent dough into 2 rectangles; press onto bottom of 13x9-inch pan sprayed with cooking spray, firmly pressing perforations and seams together to seal.
3. After that, you beat cream cheese, 3/4 cup sugar, egg white and vanilla with mixer until blended; spread onto crust.
4. Then you cover with pie filling.
5. At this point, you unroll remaining can of crescent dough; separate into 2 rectangles.
6. This is when you pat out to form 13x9-inch rectangle, pressing seams and perforations together to seal; place over pie filling.
7. Bake for about 25 to 30 min. or until golden brown; cool slightly.
8. Finally, gradually add milk to remaining sugar, beating with whisk until well blended; drizzle over dessert.

Molten Chocolate Cakes

Ingredients:

1 cup of butter

4 whole eggs

1 cup of thawed COOL WHIP Whipped Topping

2 pkg. (about 4 oz. each) BAKER'S Semi-Sweet Chocolate

2 cups of powdered sugar

4 egg yolks

12 tablespoons of flour

Directions:

1. First, you heat oven to a temperature of 425°F.
2. After which you butter 8 small custard cups; place on baking sheet.
3. After that, you microwave chocolate and butter in medium microwaveable bowl on HIGH 1 min. or until butter is melted; whisk until chocolate is completely melted.
4. At this point, you stir in sugar and add whole eggs and egg yolks; mix well.
5. Furthermore, you stir in flour and then spoon into prepared cups.
6. Bake for about 13 to 14 min. or until edges of desserts are firm but centers are still soft.
7. This is when you let stand 1 min.
8. Finally, you carefully run knife around cakes to loosen; invert into dessert plates.
9. Then you serve warm with COOL WHIP.

Meringue-Topped Southern Banana Pudding

Ingredients:

4-1/2 cups of milk

42 vanilla wafers (about 1/2 of 12-oz. pkg.)

1/3 cup of sugar

2 pkg. (about 3 oz. each) JELL-O Vanilla Flavor Cook and Serve Pudding

3 eggs (separated)

2 large bananas (sliced)

Dash cream of tartar

Directions:

1. First, you heat oven to a temperature of 350°F.
2. After which you beat pudding mixes and milk in medium saucepan with whisk until blended.
3. After that, you beat egg yolks in small bowl until blended.
4. Then you gradually stir into milk mixture.
5. This is when you bring to full rolling boil on medium heat, stirring constantly.
6. At this point, you remove from heat and arrange layer of wafers on bottom and up side of 2-qt. baking dish.
7. Furthermore, you top with layers of 1/3 of the pudding and half the banana slices.
8. After that, you repeat layers; cover with remaining pudding.
9. Then you beat egg whites and cream of tartar in medium bowl with mixer on high speed until foamy.
10. In addition, you gradually beat in sugar until stiff peaks form.
11. After which you spread over pudding, sealing to edge of dish.
12. Finally, you bake for about 15 min. or until meringue is browned. Cool.

Pumpkin Bread Pudding with Caramel Sauce

Ingredients:

8 eggs

2 can (about 15 oz. each) pumpkin

2 teaspoons of pumpkin pie spice (divided)

1 cup of chopped PLANTERS Pecans

½ cup of maple-flavored (or pancake syrup)

24 slices of cinnamon-raisin bread, cut into 1-inch cubes (about 16 cups)

2 cups of milk

2 cups plus 4 tablespoons of packed brown sugar (divided)

2 teaspoons of vanilla

1 cup of BREAKSTONE'S or KNUDSEN Sour Cream

2 cups of thawed COOL WHIP Whipped Topping

Directions:

1. First, you heat oven to a temperature of 350°F.
2. After which you place bread cubes in two 13x9-inch baking dish sprayed with cooking spray.
3. After that, you beat pumpkin, eggs, milk, 2 cup sugar, 1 teaspoon of pumpkin pie spice and vanilla with whisk until well blended.
4. Then you pour evenly over bread; sprinkle with nuts.
5. Bake for about 45 min. or until knife inserted in center comes out clean.
6. In the meantime, you mix sour cream, remaining sugar and remaining pumpkin pie spice in medium bowl until blended.
7. After that, you stir in COOL WHIP.
8. Furthermore, you drizzle syrup over pudding.
9. Finally, you serve warm topped with sour cream mixture.

Warm Caramel Bananas

Ingredients:

2/3 cup of packed brown sugar

4 bananas
1 cup of thawed COOL WHIP Whipped Topping

4 tablespoons of butter or margarine

2/3 cup of BREAKSTONE'S or KNUDSEN Sour Cream

1 cup of PLANTERS Dry Roasted Peanuts

2 oz. BAKER'S Semi-Sweet Chocolate (melted)

DIRECTIONS

1. First, you melt butter in large skillet on medium heat.
2. After which you add sugar; cook until melted, stirring occasionally.
3. After that, you gradually mix in sour cream and cook on low heat for 1 min.
4. At this point, you cut bananas lengthwise, then crosswise in half.
5. Then you add, cut sides down, to skillet; cook 1 min., basting occasionally with sauce from bottom of skillet.
6. Furthermore, you stir in nuts and spoon bananas evenly into 8 dessert dishes; top with remaining sauce in skillet.
7. Finally, you drizzle with chocolate; top with COOL WHIP.

Gingerbread People
Ingredients:

2 teaspoons of baking soda

3 teaspoons of ground cinnamon

1 ½ cups of packed brown sugar

2 egg

2 cups of powdered sugar

4 cups of flour

2 tablespoons of ground ginger

1 ½ cups of butter (softened)

2 pkg. (6.8 oz.) JELL-O Butterscotch Instant Pudding

2 tablespoons of water

Directions:

1. First, you combine the baking soda, ground cinnamon, flour, ground ginger and butter (softened).
2. After which you beat all remaining ingredients except powdered sugar and water in large bowl with mixer until blended.
3. After that, you gradually add flour mixture, mixing well after each addition and refrigerate for 1 hour.
4. Then you heat oven to a temperature of 350°F.
5. At this point, you roll out dough on lightly floured surface to 1/4-inch thickness; cut into gingerbread shapes with 4-inch cookie cutter, rerolling trimmings as necessary.
6. Furthermore, you place, 2 inches apart, on baking sheets sprayed with cooking spray.
7. Bake for about 10 to 12 min. or until edges are lightly browned.
8. In addition, you cool on baking sheets for 3 min. after which you remove to wire racks; cool completely.
9. Finally, you mix powdered sugar and water until blended.
10. After that, you use to decorate cookies as desired.

Delectable Camping Recipes

Chocolate-Candy Cane Cake

Ingredients:

1 pkg. (about 3.9 oz.) JELL-O Chocolate Instant Pudding

1 container (about 8 oz.) BREAKSTONE'S or better still KNUDSEN Sour Cream

½ cup of water

1 pkg. (about 4 oz.) BAKER'S Semi-Sweet Chocolate (chopped)

1 tub (about 8 oz.) COOL WHIP Whipped Topping (thawed)

1 pkg. (about 2-layer size) chocolate cake mix

4 eggs

½ cup of oil

¼ cup of milk

18 small candy canes, coarsely crushed (about 1 cup), divided

Directions:

1. First, you heat oven to a temperature of 350°F.
2. After which you beat JELL-O Chocolate Instant Pudding, BREAKSTONE'S or better still KNUDSEN Sour Cream, water, chocolate cake mix, eggs, oil and milk in large bowl with mixer until blended.
3. After that, you stir in chopped chocolate and 2 tablespoons of crushed candy.
4. At this point, you pour into 2 (9-inch) round pans sprayed with cooking spray.
5. Bake for about 35 to 40 min. or until toothpick inserted in centers comes out clean.
6. Then you cool in pans for about 10 min.
7. Furthermore, you loosen cakes from sides of pans; invert onto wire racks.
8. After that, you carefully remove pans and cool cakes completely.
9. Then you fill and frost cakes with COOL WHIP.
10. Finally, you sprinkle with remaining crushed candy just before serving.
11. Make sure you keep refrigerated.

Fudge-Bottom Candy Crunch Pie

Ingredients:

2 cups of cold milk

1 OREO Pie Crust

2 chocolate-covered toffee bars (about 1.4 oz. each), chopped, divided

2 pkg. (about 3.9 oz.) JELL-O Chocolate Instant Pudding

3 oz. of BAKER'S Semi-Sweet Chocolate (divided)

1 tub (about 8 oz.) COOL WHIP Whipped Topping (thawed, divided)

Directions:

1. First, you beat pudding mixes and milk in large bowl with whisk for 2 min.
2. After which you microwave 2 oz. chocolate in medium microwaveable bowl on HIGH 1 min. or until almost melted.
3. After that, you stir until completely melted. S
4. Furthermore, you stir in 1 cup pudding; pour into crust.
5. Then you add half the COOL WHIP and all but 3 Tablespoons of chopped toffee to remaining pudding; spread over pudding layer in crust.
6. At this point, you top with remaining COOL WHIP and toffee.
7. Finally, you melt remaining chocolate; drizzle over pie and refrigerate for 1 hour.

Gingerbread Pancakes with Warm Lemon Sauce

Ingredients:

2 ½ cups of warm water

5 cups of milk

2 pkg. (about 14.5 oz. each) gingerbread mix

2 eggs

2 pkg. (about 3.4 oz. each) JELL-O Lemon Flavor Instant Pudding

Directions:

1. First, you mix gingerbread mix, water and egg in large bowl until batter is smooth.
2. After which you heat griddle or large skillet sprayed with cooking spray on medium heat.
3. After that, you pour batter onto griddle, using scant ¼ cup batter for each pancake.
4. Then you cook until bubbles form on tops, then turn to brown other sides.
5. In the meantime, you beat pudding mix and milk in microwaveable bowl with whisk 2 min.
6. This is when you microwave on HIGH for 1-1/2 min. or until heated through, stirring after 1 min.
7. Finally, you serve pancakes with warm lemon sauce.

Pumpkin Bread Pudding with Caramel Sauce

Ingredients:

4 eggs

1 can (about 15 oz.) pumpkin

1 teaspoon of pumpkin pie spice (divided)

½ cup of chopped PLANTERS Pecans

¼ cup of maple-flavored (or better still pancake syrup)

12 slices cinnamon-raisin bread, cut into 1-inch cubes (about 8 cups)

1 cup of milk

1 cup plus 2 Tablespoons of packed brown sugar (divided)

1 teaspoon of vanilla

½ cup of BREAKSTONE'S or KNUDSEN Sour Cream

1 cup of thawed COOL WHIP Whipped Topping

Directions:

1. First, you heat oven to a temperature of 350°F.
2. After which you place bread cubes in 13x9-inch baking dish sprayed with cooking spray.
3. After that, you beat eggs, 1 cup sugar, milk, pumpkin, 1/2 teaspoon of pumpkin pie spice and vanilla with whisk until well blended.
4. Then you pour evenly over bread; sprinkle with nuts.
5. Bake for about 45 min. or until knife inserted in center comes out clean.
6. In the meantime, you mix sour cream, remaining sugar and remaining pumpkin pie spice in medium bowl until blended.
7. Then you stir in COOL WHIP.
8. Finally, you drizzle syrup over pudding and serve warm topped with sour cream mixture.

Chocolate Chunk Pumpkin Bread

Ingredients:

4 teaspoons of CALUMET Baking Powder

2 teaspoons of salt

1 teaspoon of ground nutmeg

2 cups of mashed cooked fresh pumpkin

1 cup of firmly packed light brown sugar

3 pkg. (about 4 oz. each) BAKER'S Semi-Sweet Chocolate (12 oz.), coarsely chopped

4 cups of flour

1 teaspoon of baking soda

2 teaspoons of ground cinnamon

4 eggs

2 cups of granulated sugar

1 cup of milk

½ cup of oil

Directions:

1. Meanwhile, you heat oven to a temperature of 350°F.
2. After which you mix flour, baking powder, baking soda, salt and spices until well blended; set aside.
3. After that, you beat eggs, sugars, pumpkin, milk and oil in large bowl with wire whisk until well blended.
4. Then you add dry ingredients; stir just until moistened.
5. This is when you stir in chopped chocolate.
6. Furthermore, you pour into two greased 9x5-inch loaf pan.
7. Bake for about 55 minutes to 1 hour or until toothpick inserted in center comes out clean and cool for 10 minutes.
8. Finally, you remove from pan; cool completely on wire rack.
9. Then you cut into 18 (1/2-inch thick) slices to serve.

Double-Chocolate Filled Strawberries

Ingredients:

½ cup of PHILADELPHIA 1/3 Less Fat than Cream Cheese

2 pkg. (about 2oz.) JELL-O White Chocolate Flavor Sugar Free Fat Free Instant Pudding

2 oz. of BAKER'S Bittersweet Chocolate

90 large fresh strawberries (about 4 lb.)

2 cups of cold fat-free milk (divided)

2 cups of thawed COOL WHIP Sugar Free Whipped Topping

2 teaspoons of lemon zest

Directions:

1. First, you cut stems off strawberries.
2. After which you cut "X" in bottom of each berry; spread pieces apart to create opening in center.
3. After that, you whisk cream cheese and ½ cup milk in medium bowl until well blended.
4. At this point, you gradually whisk in remaining milk.
5. Then you add dry pudding mix; whisk 2 min and stir in COOL WHIP and zest.
6. Furthermore, you spoon into reseal able plastic bag.
7. Finally, you cut small corner from bottom of bag; use to pipe filling into berries.
8. After that, you melt chocolate as directed; drizzle over berries.

Vanilla-Almond Fruit Tart

Ingredients:

50 vanilla wafers, about 1-3/4 cups (finely crushed)

1 pkg. (about 3.4 oz.) JELL-O Vanilla Flavor Instant Pudding

1 cup of mixed fresh fruit (such as raspberries, blueberries, blackberries, halved strawberries, sliced kiwi)

½ cup of PLANTERS Sliced Almonds (toasted, divided)

6 Tablespoons of butter (melted)

1 cup of cold milk

1 cup of thawed COOL WHIP Whipped Topping

Directions:

1. First, you reserve 1 Tablespoon of nuts.
2. After which you finely chop remaining nuts; mix with wafer crumbs and butter.
3. After that, you press onto bottom and up side of 9-inch tart pan or pie plate.
4. Then you beat pudding mix and milk with whisk 2 min.
5. This is when you stir in COOL WHIP and spoon into crust.
6. Furthermore, you refrigerate for 3 hours or until firm.
7. Finally, you top with fruit and reserved nuts just before serving.

Lemon-Blueberry Crumb Bars

Ingredients:

1 pkg. (about 2-layer size) yellow cake mix

2 pkg. (about 8 oz. each) PHILADELPHIA Cream Cheese, softened

2 ½ cups of fresh blueberries

½ cup of butter

2 eggs (divided)

½ cup of sugar

1 Tablespoon of zest and 3 Tablespoons of juice from 1 lemon

Directions:

1. First, you heat oven to a temperature of 350°F.
2. After which we line 13x9-inch pan with Reynolds Wrap® Aluminum Foil, with ends of foil extending over sides.
3. At this point, you microwave butter in large microwaveable bowl on HIGH 1 to 1-1/2 min. or until melted.
4. After that, you add dry cake mix and 1 egg; beat with mixer until blended.
5. Then you press 2/3 of the dough onto bottom of prepared pan.
6. Furthermore, you beat cream cheese and sugar with mixer until blended.
7. After which you add remaining egg, zest and juice; mix well.
8. This is when you pour over crust; top with berries.
9. In addition, you pinch small pieces of the remaining dough between your fingers; press lightly into cream cheese layer.
10. Bake for about 55 min. to 1 hour or until toothpick inserted in center comes out clean.
11. Finally, you cool completely and use foil handles to lift dessert from pan before cutting into bars.

Creamy Layered Fruit Sensation

Ingredients:

½ teaspoon of almond extract

4 pkg. (about 2oz. each) JELL-O Vanilla Flavor Sugar Free Fat Free Instant Pudding

4 pkg. (about 24 oz. each) frozen unsweetened mixed berries (such as raspberries, blueberries, sliced strawberries), thawed, well drained

6 tablespoons of orange juice

2 pkg. (about 20 oz.) prepared angel food cake, cut into 2-inch cubes

5 cups of cold fat-free milk

3 cups of thawed cool whip Sugar Free Whipped Topping (divided)

Directions:

1. First, you mix juice and extract.
2. After which you drizzle over cake cubes in large bowl and then you toss to coat.
3. After that, you heat pudding mixes and milk in a medium bowl with whisk 2 min.
4. This is when you stir in 2 cups of cool whip.
5. Then you reserve a few berries for garnish.
6. Furthermore, you place half the cake cubes in 2-qt. glass bowl; top with layers of half each of the remaining berries and pudding mixture.
7. Make sure you repeat layers.
8. After which you refrigerate for about 2 hours.
9. Finally, you top with remaining cool whip and reserved berries just before serving.

Made-Over Triple-Chocolate Dream Pie

Ingredients:

2 cups of fat-free milk

1 oz. of BAKER'S Bittersweet Chocolate (melted)

1 OREO Pie Crust (about 6 oz.)

1 pkg. (about 1.3 oz.) JELL-O Chocolate Flavor Sugar Free Fat Free Cook & Serve Pudding

2 Tablespoons of PLANTERS Creamy Peanut Butter

1-1/2 cups of thawed COOL WHIP FREE Whipped Topping (divided)

Directions:

1. First, you cook pudding mix with milk in large saucepan as directed on package.
2. After which, you remove from heat and whisk in peanut butter.
3. After that, you place pan in bowl of ice water; let stand for about 5 min., stirring occasionally.
4. In the meantime, you whisk chocolate and 1/3 cup COOL WHIP until blended; spread onto bottom of pie crust.
5. Then you add 2/3 cup of the remaining COOL WHIP to pudding; whisk until blended.
6. At this point, you pour into crust.
7. Furthermore, you refrigerate for 3 hours or until firm.
8. After which, you serve topped with remaining COOL WHIP.

Chocolate Dunk Cookies

Ingredients:

1 ½ teaspoons of baking soda

2 pkg. (about 4 oz. each) BAKER'S Semi-Sweet Chocolate, divided

1 cup of packed brown sugar

2 eggs

2 teaspoons of warm water

3 ½ cups of flour

½ teaspoon of salt

1 ½ cups (about 3 sticks) margarine, softened

1 cup of granular no-calorie sweetener

2 teaspoons of vanilla

2 tablespoons of thawed COOL WHIP Sugar Free Whipped Topping

Directions:

1. First, you heat oven to a temperature of 375°F.
2. After that, you mix flour, baking soda and salt.
3. After which you chop 4 oz. chocolate.
4. At this point, you beat margarine, brown sugar and granulated sweetener in large bowl with mixer until light and fluffy.
5. This is when you blend in egg and vanilla.
6. Then you gradually beat in flour mixture and stir in chopped chocolate.
7. Furthermore, you drop heaping tablespoonful of dough, 2 inches apart, onto baking sheets.
8. Bake for about 11 to 12 min. or until lightly browned.
9. After that, you cool on baking sheets for 1 min.; remove to wire racks and cool completely.
10. In addition, you melt remaining chocolate as directed on package.
11. Finally, you stir in COOL WHIP and water.
12. Make sure you dip half of each cookie in chocolate; let stand until firm.

Low-Fat Chocolate-Banana Parfaits

Ingredients:

4 cups of cold fat-free milk

1 ½ cup of thawed COOL WHIP LITE Whipped Topping (divided)

2 pkg. (about 2.8 oz.) JELL-O Chocolate Sugar Free Fat Free Instant Pudding

4 bananas (sliced)

Directions:

1. First, you beat pudding mix and milk with whisk 2 min.
2. After which you spoon half the pudding evenly into 4 dessert glasses; cover with layers of bananas and half the COOL WHIP.
3. After that, you top with remaining pudding and COOL WHIP.
4. Finally, you refrigerate for 1 hour.

DELECTABLE SIDE DISH RECIPE

Hoisin Honey Chicken Wings

Ingredients

2 tablespoons of hoisin sauce

1 tablespoon of sesame oil

1 teaspoon of ginger (minced)

1 tablespoon of toasted sesame seeds

1 18x18-inch sheet of Reynolds Wrap Heavy Duty Aluminum Foil

6 split of chicken wings

1 tablespoon of soy sauce

1 tablespoon of honey

Salt and pepper (to taste)

½ cup of green onions (chopped)

Directions

1. First, you toss split chicken wing in a large bowl, hoisin sauce, soy sauce, sesame oil, honey, ginger and salt and pepper.
2. After which you place on an 18x18-inch sheet of Reynolds Wrap® Heavy Duty Aluminum Foil.
3. After that, you form a packet.
4. Then you grill over high heat, turning once, about 30 minutes.
5. At this point, you carefully open packet and top with green onions and sesame seeds.
6. Then you serve.

Slow-Roasted Potato Salad with Bacon

Ingredients

4 strips bacon (cut in 1/4-inch strips)

1 ½ tablespoons of olive oil

1 tablespoon of apple cider vinegar

4 scallions, sliced (reserve some to finish on top)

2 pounds of new potatoes (halved)

¼ teaspoon of sea salt (plus more for finishing)

½ cup of sour cream

1 ½ tablespoons of coarse mustard

Pepper

Directions

1. Meanwhile, you heat grill on high.
2. After which you lay three pieces of Reynolds Wrap® Aluminum Foil on top of one another.
3. After that, you add the potatoes, ¼ teaspoon salt, olive oil and bacon.
4. Then you make a packet and seal tightly.
5. At this point, you grill for about 45 minutes to 1 hour, flipping the packet every 15 minutes.
6. Furthermore, you grill until the potatoes are tender and the bacon and potatoes are browned in parts.
7. After that, you let the potatoes cool for about 10 minutes before adding them to a large bowl.
8. Then add the sour cream, coarse mustard, cider vinegar, and scallions and toss to combine.
9. This is when you season with salt and pepper.
10. Finally, you place the potato salad in a serving bowl, then garnish with reserved scallions. Serve.

Mexican Spiced Corn Packets

Ingredients

2 tablespoons of butter

½ cup of sour cream

2 teaspoons of chili powder

Salt to taste

18x18-inch sheet of Reynolds Wrap® Heavy Duty Aluminum Foil

8 ears corn

½ cup of mayonnaise

½ cup of crumbled cotija cheese

Juice and zest from 2 lime

½ cup cilantro (chopped)

Lime wedges

Directions

1. First, you cut kernels of corn.
2. After which you mix together in a bowl the corn kernels, sour cream, coria cheese, butter, mayonnaise, chili powder and lime juice and zest.
3. After that, you season with salt and pepper to taste.
4. Then you place corn mixture on an 18x18-inch sheet of Reynolds Wrap® Heavy Duty Aluminum Foil.
5. At this point, you form a packet.
6. Furthermore, you grill over high heat for about 25 minutes (carefully open packet).
7. Finally, you top with cilantro and serve with lime wedges.

Potato Salad

Ingredients

12 small diced hard-boiled eggs

1 small large yellow onion, diced

Salt and pepper to taste

12 pounds of red potatoes (cut into 8 wedges)

1 medium diced stalk of celery (with leaves removed)

½ cup of Dijon mustard

1 ½ cups of mayonnaise

Directions

1. First, you cook the cut potatoes in a large pot of boiling salted water for about 20 minutes.
2. After which you immediately strain the hot water and shock the potatoes with ice to chill them.
3. After that, you strain the potatoes and add it to a large bowl along with the diced hard-boiled eggs, onion, celery, mayonnaise, mustard, salt and pepper and mix thoroughly until combined.
4. Then you transfer the tossed potato salad to a Reynolds® Large Bakeware Pan and chill before serving.

Delightfully Light Green Bean Casserole

Ingredients

4 tablespoons of butter

2 (20 3/4-ounce) can reduced-fat and reduced-sodium cream of mushroom soup

½ cup bottled roasted red sweet peppers, chopped, or better still 1 (4-ounce jar) diced pimiento, drained

6 (9-ounce) packages frozen French-cut green beans (thawed and drained)

2 medium onion (finely chopped 1 cup)

2/3 cup of finely crushed rich round crackers (or better still fine dry bread crumbs)

½ cup of slivered almonds

½ teaspoon of salt

½ teaspoon of ground black pepper

Directions

1. Meanwhile, you heat oven to a temperature of 350°F.
2. After which you line a 2-quart casserole with Reynolds Wrap® Non-Stick Foil.
3. After that, you cook onion in hot butter over medium heat until tender in a small saucepan.
4. Then you remove from heat and then stir in crushed crackers; set aside.
5. At this point, you combine soup, almonds, roasted peppers, salt, and black pepper in a large bowl.
6. This is when you stir in green beans.
7. Furthermore, you transfer mixture to prepared casserole.
8. After which you sprinkle with cracker mixture.
9. Finally, you bake uncovered, for about 30 to 35 minutes or until heated through.
10. Makes 12 servings.

Baked Pesto Chicken Sandwich

Ingredients

½ cup of pesto

8 ciabatta rolls (sliced)

8 slices of provolone cheese

4 cups of shredded rotisserie-cooked chicken

6 tablespoons of light mayonnaise

8 ounces roasted red peppers, cut in strips (approx. 2 roasted red peppers)

Directions

1. Meanwhile, you heat oven to 350oF degrees.
2. After which you tear off four 12 x 12-inch sheets of Reynolds Wrap® Aluminum Foil.
3. After that, you mix chicken, mayo, pesto, salt and pepper in a medium bowl.
4. Then you spread equal portions of the chicken mixture onto bottom half of each roll.
5. At this point you top with roasted red peppers and cheese.
6. Furthermore, you place top of bread on each sandwich and then wrap in foil sheets.
7. After that, you place wrapped sandwiches on a baking sheet.
8. Finally, you bake for about 20 minutes and then you serve immediately or keep warm at 200oF.

Slow Cooker Honey Apple Challah Stuffing

Ingredients

5 cups of apples (seeded and chopped)

3 cups of apple juice
5 Tablespoons of unsalted butter
1 teaspoon of kosher salt

8 cups of challah bread (about 1 loaf) cut into about 1" cubes

1 cup of white onion chopped

1 cup of fresh parsley chopped

½ cup of honey (plus extra for drizzling, if desired)

1 teaspoon of all spice

Directions

1. First, you line slow cooker insert with a Reynolds® Slow Cooker Liner and place into slow cooker base.
2. After which you set the slow cooker to high heat and add onion and butter.
3. Then once butter is melted and the onions start to warm up, add in apples, all spice, salt and honey.
4. After that, you add apple juice and let cook for about 5 minutes.
5. This is when you top mixture with challah cubes and parsley.
6. At this point, you cover the slow cooker and let cook for about 30 minutes on LOW.
7. Furthermore, you stir the ingredients, cover, and continue to cook on low setting.
8. After that, you cook for 4 more hours.
9. Then you remove lid in the last hour of cooking time.
10. Finally, you turn off slow cooker completely, transfer stuffing into a serving dish and drizzle with additional honey (if desired), discard slow cooker liner and serve.

Layered Taco Dip
Ingredients

2 cups of chopped rotisserie chicken

2 teaspoons of olive oil

2 packet of taco seasoning

12 ounces of shredded jack cheese

½ cup of sliced green onions

1 pound of cooked and chopped chorizo

1 small diced sweet onion

4 cans of refried pinto beans

8 ounces of shredded cheddar cheese

½ cup of diced tomatoes

Directions

1. Meanwhile, you heat the oven to 350°
2. After which you cook the onions on medium heat in olive oil for 4 to 6 minutes or until slightly brown.
3. After that, you add in the taco seasoning and pinto beans and stir.
4. At this point, you layer the Reynolds® 8x8 Bakeware pan as followed: refried beans and cooked onions, cheddar cheese, ½ of the jack cheese, chopped chicken, chorizo, and the rest of the jack cheese.
5. Then you place the pan in the oven and bake for 25 minutes.
6. Finally, you finish the dip with diced tomatoes and green onions.

Vegetarian Black Bean Soup

Ingredients

2 medium sweet potatoes (peeled and cut into 1-inch pieces)

1 medium red sweet pepper (seeded and coarsely chopped)

1 medium onion (coarsely chopped)

1 ½ tablespoons of chili powder

Shredded cheddar cheese (it is optional)

2 cans (about 15 to 16 ounces each) black beans (rinsed and drained)

2 cups of orange juice

1 cup of packaged peeled fresh baby carrots, bias-sliced crosswise

1 jalapeño Chile pepper (seeded and finely chopped)

1 teaspoon of ground cumin

1 clove garlic (minced)

Directions

1. First, you line a 5- to 6-quart slow cooker with a Reynolds® Slow Cooker Liner.
2. After which you add beans, sweet pepper, chili powder, sweet potatoes, orange juice, carrots, onion, jalapeño pepper, cumin, and garlic to the prepared slow cooker.
3. After that, you stir gently with a rubber spatula to combine.
4. Then you cover and cook for 4 hours on high or for 8 hours on low.
5. Finally you serve with cheese, if desired.

Homemade Spinach Pizza Rolls

Ingredients

8 ounces bulk Italian sausage

1 cup of shredded mozzarella cheese (about 4 ounces), divided

¼ cup of grated Parmesan cheese

1 can (about 8 ounces) pizza sauce (warmed)

1 tablespoon of cornmeal

1 package (about 13.8 ounces) refrigerated pizza dough

1 cup of fresh baby spinach

1 egg (lightly beaten)

Directions

1. First, you heat oven to a temperature of 375°F.
2. After which you line a large baking sheet with Reynolds Wrap Non-Stick Aluminum Foil; sprinkle with cornmeal. Set aside.
3. After that, you brown sausage in large skillet on medium-high heat.
4. At this point, you drain and set aside.
5. This is when you unroll pizza dough onto prepared baking sheet.
6. Then you carefully stretch or roll dough into a 13x10-inch rectangle.
7. Furthermore, you arrange sausage on dough to within 1/2 inch of the edges.
8. After that, you sprinkle with 1/2 cup of the mozzarella and layer spinach on cheese.
9. In addition, you top with the remaining 1/2 cup mozzarella and the Parmesan.
10. After which you starting from a long side, roll up dough to make a 13-inch-long loaf. Pinch seam and ends to seal.
11. After that, you loaf, seam side down, on the prepared baking sheet and then brush with egg.
12. Using a sharp knife, you cut four 2-inch slits in top for steam to escape.

13. Bake for about 20 to 25 minutes or until golden brown (If necessary, you cover the last 5 minutes of baking to prevent overbrowning).
14. Finally, you remove from oven and slice into rounds to serve with pizza sauce.

CONCLUSION

As long as you adhere to the advice that was outlined from this article everything should work out for you while you go camping. Camping is a once in a lifetime experience, and will help you relax

Delectable Camping Recipes

www.ingramcontent.com/pod-product-compliance
Lightning Source LLC
Chambersburg PA
CBHW081726100526
44591CB00016B/2516